PRESIDENTS' DAY

BY TRUDI STRAIN TRUEIT · ILLUSTRATED BY MICHELLE DORENKAMP

Published in the United States of America by The Child's World®
1980 Lookout Drive • Mankato, MN 56003-1705
800-599-READ • www.childsworld.com

ACKNOWLEDGMENTS

The Child's World®: Mary Berendes, Publishing Director

The Design Lab: Kathleen Petelinsek, Design; Julia Goozen, Page Production

Editorial Direction: Red Line Editorial, Patricia Stockland, Managing Editor

LIBRARY OF CONGRESS CATALOGING-IN-PUBLICATION DATA

Trueit, Trudi Strain.
   Presidents' Day / by Trudi Strain Trueit ; illustrated by
Michelle Dorenkamp.
      p. cm. — (Holidays, festivals & celebrations)
   Includes bibliographical references and index.
   Audience: Grades K-3.
   ISBN-13: 978-1-59296-816-9 (library bound : alk. paper)
   ISBN-10: 1-59296-816-3 (library bound : alk. paper)
   1. Presidents' Day—Juvenile literature. 2. Presidents—United
States—History—Juvenile literature. I. Dorenkamp, Michelle. II.
Title. III. Series.
   E176.8.T78 2007
   394.261—dc22   2006103482

TABLE OF CONTENTS

CHAPTER ONE

PRIDE AND PRESIDENTS

The American President resembles the commander of a ship at sea. He must have a helm to grasp, a course to steer, a port to seek.
—Henry Adams (1838–1918), grandson and great-grandson of U.S. presidents John Quincy Adams and John Adams

People crowd the sidewalks of Old Town Alexandria, Virginia. A marching band plays "Yankee Doodle." Here comes a red, white, and blue float. You're just in time for the Presidents' Day parade!

Presidents' Day falls on the third Monday in February. The holiday honors the presidents of the United States, especially George Washington (1732–1799) and Abraham Lincoln (1809–1865). Both of these leaders were born in February.

So wave an American flag and join the celebration!

Join the parade for Presidents' Day!

CHAPTER TWO

NEVER GIVE UP!

G eorge Washington was born on February 22, 1732, in Virginia Colony. As a boy, George dreamed of being a soldier. When he was 21 years old, George joined the Virginia **militia**.

In 1759, George married Martha Custis. They settled on George's Virginia farm called Mount Vernon. Their quiet life didn't last long.

Did you know the story about young George Washington chopping down a cherry tree isn't true? It was made up by a writer.

George and Martha Washington were farmers in the colonies.

The colonies were tired of obeying Great Britain. The colonists wanted to be free to rule themselves. In 1775, British and American soldiers started shooting at each other. The Revolutionary War (1775–1783) had begun!

George Washington led the colonial forces into battle. His small Continental Army was no match for the mighty British. Yet, Washington did not give up. The winter of 1778 was very cold in Valley Forge, Pennsylvania. The Continental Army didn't have enough food or supplies. On February 22nd, the troops celebrated General Washington's birthday (he was 46). They played music and sang. It lifted everyone's spirits.

In time, Washington's patience and clever battle plans paid off. The colonies won the war!

Celebrating General Washington's birthday cheered up the troops.

"Liberty, when it begins to take root, is a plant of rapid growth."
—*George Washington*

CHAPTER THREE

FATHER OF HIS COUNTRY

I often say of George Washington that he was one of the few in the whole history of the world who was not carried away by power.
—Robert Frost (1874–1963), American poet

At last, the United States was **independent**! The new nation needed a leader. Again, people turned to Washington. Some wanted to crown him king of the country. Washington said "no." The country needed a citizen to guide it, not a king to rule it.

In 1789, Washington was chosen to be the first U.S. president. Soon, it became a **tradition** for American cities to celebrate his birthday.

Washington was a kind leader. He was against slavery. He felt land had been wrongly taken from Native Americans. He tried to help them. After two terms (eight years), Washington went home to Virginia.

On December 14, 1799, George Washington died at Mount Vernon. The United States lost a brave hero, founding father, and beloved president.

"A citizen, first in war, first in peace, first in the hearts of his countryman."
—General Henry Lee (1732–1794)

President Washington was a fair and kind leader.

CHAPTER FOUR

HONEST ABE

Abraham Lincoln was born in a log cabin in Kentucky on February 12, 1809. Young Abe loved reading. One of his favorite books was about George Washington.

Abe was bright, funny, and honest. His good **character** got him elected to the state **legislature** in 1834. He began speaking out against slavery. In 1842, Abe married Mary Todd.

Abraham Lincoln read as many books as he could find.

"A house divided against itself cannot stand. I believe this government cannot endure permanently half slave and half free."
—Abraham Lincoln, 1858 campaign speech

In 1860, Lincoln became the sixteenth president of the United States. By now, the issue of slavery was splitting the nation. The South wanted to withdraw from the United States to form its own country. Lincoln was determined not to let that happen. This led to the Civil War (1861–1865). In 1863, Lincoln freed the slaves. But it took two more years for the North to win the war.

Lincoln was elected to a second term. On April 14, 1865, he was shot by John Wilkes Booth. Booth supported the South. He was angry about the war. Lincoln died the next morning.

Today, Lincoln is remembered as a strong president. He kept the United States together during one of its hardest times.

Abraham Lincoln was the tallest U.S. President. He was six feet, four inches tall—about one inch taller than George Washington!

The Civil War was the bloodiest war in U.S. history.

The U.S. Civil War lasted from 1861 to 1865. For four long years, the war divided the nation. The northern states and the southern states fought each other over the issue of slavery. The war divided families and friends. Thousands of people died. If the North hadn't won the war, the South could have become a separate country and slavery could have continued there.

CHAPTER FIVE

A NATION CELEBRATES

I n 1885, U.S. President Chester Arthur declared Washington's birthday a national holiday. By now, some states were observing Abraham Lincoln's birthday, too (though it was never made a U.S. holiday).

In 1968, the U.S. **Congress** moved Washington's birthday celebration to the third Monday in February. It became more commonly known as Presidents' Day, a holiday to honor *all* presidents.

Government offices, banks, and schools close on Presidents' Day. People fly U.S. flags. There are parades, concerts, plays, and fireworks shows. Some people lay wreaths at the Washington Monument

Many U.S. monuments and memorials honor former presidents.

Mount Rushmore in South Dakota is one of the most famous memorials to U.S. presidents. The heads of George Washington, Thomas Jefferson, Abraham Lincoln, and Theodore Roosevelt are carved into a granite cliff. Each face is 60 feet tall!

and the Lincoln Memorial in Washington, D.C. Thousands of people show up to pay their respects at Mount Vernon!

It is also tradition for a senator to read George Washington's 1796 farewell address to Congress. The Father of His Country gave the nation and its people some wise advice. "Observe good faith and justice toward all nations; cultivate peace and harmony with all."

PRESIDENTS' FACES ON U.S. MONEY:

Washington is on the quarter and the one dollar bill.

Lincoln is on the penny and the five dollar bill.

Thomas Jefferson is on the nickel.

Franklin Roosevelt is on the dime.

Andrew Jackson is on the twenty dollar bill.

CHAPTER SIX

HAIL TO THE CHIEF

PRESIDENTIAL OATH OF OFFICE:

"I do solemnly swear that I will faithfully execute the office of President of the United States, and will to the best of my ability, preserve, protect, and defend the Constitution of the United States."

D o you ever wonder what the president does? He or she works with Congress to create laws. The president meets with world leaders to keep peace. The president commands the military in times of war.

The United States has had more than forty presidents. Each one has been different. Thomas Jefferson was born into a rich family. Abraham Lincoln was very poor. Before taking the Oath of Office, Harry Truman ran a clothing store. Jimmy Carter owned a peanut farm. Ronald Reagan was a movie actor.

That is a wonderful thing about the United States. Any citizen who was born in the country can be president.

Before becoming president, Jimmy Carter grew peanuts!

There are advantages to
being elected President.
The day after I was elected,
I had my high school grades
classified Top Secret.
—Ronald Reagan
(1911–2004),
40th U.S. President

CHAPTER SEVEN

POETRY CORNER

A Nation's Strength

What makes a nation's pillars high
And its foundations strong?
What makes it mighty to defy
The foes that round it throng?

Brave men who work while others sleep,
Who dare while others fly . . .
They build a nation's pillars deep
And lift them to the sky.
—Ralph Waldo Emerson
(1803–1882), American poet

The ultimate rulers of
our democracy are not a
President and senators
and congressmen and
government officials, but the
voters of this country.
—Franklin D. Roosevelt
(1882–1945),
32nd U.S. President

Praise for a Nation

My country owes me nothing.
It gave me, as it gives to every boy and girl, a chance.
It gave me schooling, independence of action,
opportunity for service and honor.
In no other land could a boy from a country village,
without inheritance or influential friends, look
forward with unbounded hope.
—Herbert Hoover (1874–1964),
  31st U.S. President

Let every nation know,
whether it wishes us well
or ill, that we shall pay any
price, bear any burden, meet
any hardship, support any
friend, oppose any foe to
assure the survival and the
success of liberty.
—John F. Kennedy
  (1917–1963),
  35th U.S. President

CHAPTER EIGHT

SONGS OF PRESIDENTS' DAY

Hail to the Chief

Hail to the Chief we have chosen for the nation, hail to the Chief! We salute him, one and all. Hail to the Chief, as we pledge co-operation, in proud fulfillment of a great, noble call. Yours is the aim to make this grand country grander, this you will do; that's our strong, firm belief. Hail to the one we selected as commander, hail to the President! Hail to the Chief!
—*traditional lyrics*

Any time the president attends an important event, the song "Hail to the Chief" is played in his or her honor. This tradition began in the early 1800s. The song is also played at a president's funeral.

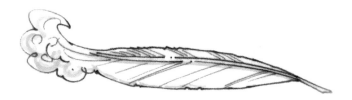

Yankee Doodle Dandy

Father and I went down to camp
Along with Captain Gooding,
And there we saw the men and boys
As thick as hasty pudding.

Chorus:
Yankee doodle, keep it up
Yankee doodle dandy
Mind the music and the step
And with the girls be handy.

There was Captain Washington
Upon a slapping stallion
A-giving orders to his men,
I guess there was a million.
—traditional lyrics

My Country 'Tis of Thee

My country 'tis of thee, sweet land of liberty, of thee I sing;
Land where my fathers died, land of the pilgrims' pride,
from every mountain side let freedom ring.

My native country, thee, land of the noble free, thy name I love;
I love thy rocks and rills, thy woods and templed hills;
My heart with rapture thrills like that above.
—words by Samuel Francis Smith (1808–1895),
  minister

The pay is good and I can walk to work.
—John F. Kennedy

Joining in the Spirit of Presidents' Day

- Imagine that you are the president of the United States! Make a list of some things you would work to accomplish. What would you change? How would you do it?

- Who is your favorite president and why? Write a poem or song in his honor.

- Ask a parent or grandparent about a president they remember from their childhood. What was America like when they were young? What challenges did the nation have to overcome?

- Write a thank-you letter to the president of the United States. Send it to:

    The White House

    1600 Pennsylvania Avenue N.W.

    Washington, D.C. 20500

- Go to a Presidents' Day parade, concert, or play and have fun!

Making a Cherry Pie

It may be just a legend that George Washington chopped down a cherry tree. But you can still enjoy a slice of warm cherry pie on Presidents' Day. Be sure to have an adult help you.

What you need:

1 box of pre-made refrigerated pie crust (comes with two crusts)
2 cans of cherry pie filling

Directions:

Pre-heat oven to 400 degrees Fahrenheit. Roll out one of the pre-made crusts and place it into the bottom of a 9-inch pie plate. Pour both cans of cherry pie filling into the pie crust. Even out the filling with a spoon. Place the second pie crust on top of the pie. Seal the edges of the two crusts together. Going around the outside of the pie plate, press a fork into the edge of the dough (an adult can help you with this). With a knife, cut a small cross into the center of the pie to release steam during baking. Place the pie on a cookie sheet. Bake for 40 to 45 minutes until the crust is golden brown and the filling is bubbling. After baking, let the pie cool before serving. Serve your cherry pie alone or à la mode (that means with a scoop of your favorite ice cream!).

Log Cabin Crafts

On Presidents' Day, make some log cabin crafts in honor of Abraham Lincoln. You'll find all of the ingredients in your kitchen.

What you need:

A ½ pint milk carton, washed thoroughly
Creamy peanut butter
Pretzels, graham crackers, wheat crackers, cereal squares
Scissors

Directions:

Spread the outside of the milk carton with creamy peanut butter. The pretzels will be the logs on the walls of the house. Using the scissors, cut the pretzel sticks the same length as the width of the cabin. Now lay the sticks side by side on the peanut butter. Using the cereal squares, add windows and a door. Using the crackers, make the roof.

Voilà! A log cabin!

Words to Know

character—the quality of an individual's personality or reputation

Congress—the national legislature of the U.S. made up of the House and Senate; the elected people who make U.S. laws

independent—free; not under the control of others

legislature—an elected group of lawmakers

militia—citizens trained to fight as soldiers in an emergency

slavery—a system where people are forced to work for others

tradition—a long-held custom

How to Learn More about Presidents' Day

At the Library

Collier, James Lincoln. *The Abraham Lincoln You Never Knew.* New
    York: Children's Press, 2003.

Roop, Peter. *Let's Celebrate Presidents' Day.* Brookfield, CT: Millbrook
    Press, 2001.

Venezia, Mike. *George Washington: First President, 1789-1797.* New
    York: Children's Press, 2004.

Wade, Mary Dodson. *Presidents' Day: Honoring the Birthdays
    of Washington and Lincoln.* Berkeley Heights, NJ: Enslow
    Publishers, 2004.

On the Web

Visit our Web site for lots of links about Presidents' Day:
http://www.childsworld.com/links
NOTE TO PARENTS, TEACHERS, AND LIBRARIANS:
We routinely verify our Web links to make sure they're safe,
active sites—so encourage your readers to check them out!

ABOUT THE AUTHOR

Trudi Strain Trueit is a former television news reporter and anchor. She has written more than forty books for children. She lives in Everett, Washington, with her husband, Bill, a teacher.

ABOUT THE ILLUSTRATOR

Michelle Dorenkamp has a BFA in Graphic Design/ Illustration. To date, she has illustrated more than fifty children's books for various publishers around the world. She lives in St. Louis, Missouri, and enjoys spending free time with her family—especially her granddaughter Katlyn!

Index

GAYLORD   PRINTED IN U.S.A.

FEB 2 4 2009

DATE DUE